RUTH AND JUDITH

RUTH AND JUDITH

Introduced by

JOAN CHITTISTER

DARTON·LONGMAN+TODD

This edition of the Books of Ruth and Judith first published in 2010 by
Darton, Longman and Todd Ltd
1 Spencer Court
140-142 Wandsworth High Street
London SW18 4JJ

Nihil obstat Anthony Cowan
Imprimatur Rt Rev John Crowley V. G. Bishop in Central London
Westminster 4ᵗʰ September 1989

The Nihil obstat *and* Imprimatur *are a declaration that a book or pamphlet is
considered to be free from doctrinal or moral error. It is not implied that those who
have granted the Nihil obstat and Imprimatur agree with the contents, opinions or
statements expressed.*

ISBN 978-0-232-52803-9

A catalogue record for this book is available from the British Library.

Produced by Judy Linard
Printed and bound in Great Britain by Thomson Litho, East Kilbride,
Scotland

INTRODUCTION

Joan Chittister

Finding role models to live by in Scripture, if you are a woman, is slim picking. I spent a fair amount of my young life looking for them, in fact. I heard a great deal in church and school about the kings, Solomon and David. They taught us about the faithful ones like Job and Joseph, for instance, who, despite their sufferings, never cursed God. But they said precious little, hardly a word, about women. Except about Delilah, of course, who had tempted Samson, leading to his ruin, and about Eve, who had tempted Adam and left us all in ruin.

Such teaching left girls with very male images of what it meant to be loved by God, or chosen by God, or 'made in the image of' God. Abraham and

Moses and any number of other men – such as Noah, Jacob, Daniel, Isaac, Joshua and Isaiah, to name just a few – had been entrusted with the work of God. But you didn't hear much about women at all, except, of course, for Mary, 'the mother of God', who was clearly too exalted, too divinised, to be a real model for real women. Women, it seemed, were also-rans when the work of salvation was concerned.

It takes years for a woman to realise how effective, how distorting, that exclusion can be to her sense of herself before God. What became clear to me, over the years, is that men got us to heaven; women went along. Men were the doers of God's will; women were everybody's 'helpmates', but never their leaders. Women, in fact, were seldom or never the carriers of the vision. They were almost never the speakers of God's word. I admit to being disappointed by it all.

How was it that God preferred men to women in the great economy of salvation? My teachers blamed Eve, of course, but the Scripture is clear: 'While they were in the garden together ...'.

'Together,' I remember reading. Adam was there, too.

Why didn't he stop the process, if he was so much holier than she was? After all, Scripture says that they both ate of the apple; Adam – big, strong, rational, chosen Adam – ate of it, too. And he did it on the word of someone suggested to be weaker than he to begin with. My teachers said not a word about his responsibility to make up his own mind about things, of course; only about her responsibility not to state her own ideas. It was a huge spiritual conundrum.

As a result, I did what most girls did. I looked to male figures and male saints and male spiritual leaders, for direction, for the interpretation of what, if anything, God expected of me in life. But, somehow or other, little or none of it fitted. Worse, all of it reminded me of a woman's secondary status, even where God was concerned. There was something not right about that.

Then, one day, I discovered, almost by accident, the books of Ruth and Judith – two women who were strong leaders and committed followers of the Word of God. But these books had never been read in my church. I had never heard anyone even preach a sermon on them. I never saw any pictures of these two women hanging anywhere on sacred territory. But there were their stories, full and entire, right in the middle of the Bible. They were not pieces of religious fancy. These were, the priest told me, solemnly, 'the Word of God'. Suddenly, things began to change.

There are few books in Scripture that are dedicated to the witness of a single person. But there, with the likes of Job and Jonah, Solomon and David, the books of Ruth and Judith stand as witnesses to the place of women in the economy of salvation. From those two books, we get a completely different image of the place of women before the face of God.

Ruth is an immigrant woman, whose strength comes from another woman, Naomi, the mother of Ruth's deceased husband. Completely alone in life, Ruth and Naomi set out together to hew out a new life for themselves in a strange land. They travel the roads alone, settle in a foreign territory alone, make their own living and develop the connections it took, not only to survive, but to continue the family lineage. It is this lineage of Naomi's, and the marriage of Ruth and Boaz, from which will come Jesus and the promise of salvation for us all. No small accomplishment.

But, more than that, it is in the Book of Ruth that, for the first time in Scripture, women name the child that will continue the line of David. Most telling of all, in the last chapter of the book, Boaz, father of the child, is not present at all. It is the women of the village who place the baby between the legs of the old woman Naomi, to indicate her role in driving the narrative of the Will of God to fulfillment.

In the Book of Ruth, both women and men can see the twelve great moments in every woman's life through which women come to full spiritual maturity and adult agency in the bringing of the Word of God. In this book, women are not handmaids only, or dependents only, or helpmates only. They are moral agents of the Holy Spirit. They save the line of David as surely as Moses, or any other man, had part in saving the people before them. To these women, God entrusts the work of the history of salvation for us all.

In the Book of Judith, a woman rises up again to save the people. She rouses the male leaders of the city, who have gone weak and soft, frightened and submissive, to resist the enemy to which they were prepared to surrender. Judith knows both her

womanhood and her strength. She uses her brains
rather than her brawn, and saves both the people of
God and the army of the enemy. She calls on God
to strengthen her woman's arm and give her the
power she needs to forego force with faith.

The books of Ruth and Judith are two great
stories about God's obvious work with women,
through women, for the sake of the entire human
community.

If anything in Scripture prepares us for the
Jesus who walked with women, taught women,
and commissioned women, these stories are
surely it. They prepare us to see, if only we will
open our eyes, the place and power of women in
the Work of God. They enable us to realise the
message of redemptive presence that comes
through the stories of the women around Jesus –
Mary, Mary Magdalen, the Samaritan woman, the
woman in the house of the Pharisees and all the
women of all the house churches in the New
Testament.

The books of Ruth and Judith are signs to us
all. They are signs to men of the ministry, that they
must share equally with women. They are signs to
women of the ministry, for which they, too, must

take clear and conscious responsibility, knowing, indeed, that God is with them, in them, calling them on, as witnesses, ministers and leaders – for all our sakes.

Publisher's Note: The book of Judith is one of a handful of books of the Bible that do not appear in some editions. Some Christians consider the books, known as the 'Deuterocanonicals', not to be part of official scriptural canon.

RUTH

RUTH AND NAOMI

1 In the days when the Judges were governing, a famine occurred in the country and a certain man from Bethlehem of Judah went—he, his wife and his two sons—to live in the Plains of Moab. ²The man was called Elimelech, his wife Naomi and his two sons Mahlon and Chilion; they were Ephrathites from Bethlehem of Judah. Going to the Plains of Moab, they settled there. ³Elimelech, Naomi's husband, died, and she and her two sons were left. ⁴These married Moabite women: one was called Orpah and the other Ruth. They lived there for about ten years. ⁵Mahlon and Chilion then both died too, and Naomi was thus bereft of her two sons and her husband. ⁶She then decided to come back from the Plains of Moab with her daughters-in-law, having heard in the Plains of Moab that God had visited his people and given them food. ⁷So, with her daughters-in-law, she left the place where she was living and they took the road back to Judah.

⁸Naomi said to her two daughters-in-law, 'Go back, each of you to your mother's house. ⁹May Yahweh show you faithful love, as you have done to those who have died and to me. Yahweh grant that you may each find happiness with a husband!' She then kissed them, but they began weeping loudly, ¹⁰and said, 'No, we shall go back with you to your people.' ¹¹'Go home, daughters,' Naomi replied. 'Why come with me? Have I any more sons in my womb to make husbands for you? ¹²Go home, daughters, go, for I am now too old to marry again. Even if I said, "I still have a hope: I shall take a husband this very night and shall bear more sons," ¹³would you be prepared to wait for them until they were grown up? Would you refuse to marry for their sake? No, daughters, I am bitterly sorry for your sakes that the hand of Yahweh should have been raised against me.' ¹⁴They started weeping loudly all over again; Orpah then kissed her mother-in-law and went back to her people. But Ruth stayed with her.

¹⁵Naomi then said, 'Look, your sister-in-law has

gone back to her people and to her god. Go home, too; follow your sister-in-law.'

¹⁶But Ruth said, 'Do not press me to leave you and to stop going with you, for

> wherever you go, I shall go,
> wherever you live, I shall live.
> Your people will be my people,
> and your God will be my God.
> ¹⁷ Where you die, I shall die
> and there I shall be buried.
> Let Yahweh bring unnameable ills on me
> and worse ills, too,
> if anything but death
> should part me from you!'

¹⁸Seeing that Ruth was determined to go with her, Naomi said no more.

¹⁹The two of them went on until they came to Bethlehem. Their arrival set the whole town astir, and the women said, 'Can this be Naomi?' ²⁰To this she replied, 'Do not call me Naomi, call me Mara, for Shaddai has made my lot bitter.

> ²¹ I departed full,

and Yahweh has brought me home empty.
Why, then, call me Naomi,
since Yahweh has pronounced against me
and Shaddai has made me wretched?'

²²This was how Naomi came home with her daughter-in-law, Ruth the Moabitess, on returning from the Plains of Moab. They arrived in Bethlehem at the beginning of the barley harvest.

RUTH IN THE FIELD OF BOAZ

2 Naomi had a kinsman on her husband's side, well-to-do and of Elimelech's clan. His name was Boaz.

²Ruth the Moabitess said to Naomi, 'Let me go into the fields and glean ears of corn in the footsteps of some man who will look on me with favour.' She replied, 'Go, daughter.' ³So she set out and went to glean in the fields behind the reapers. Chance led her to a plot of land belonging to Boaz of Elimelech's clan. ⁴Boaz, as it happened, had just

come from Bethlehem. 'Yahweh be with you!' he said to the reapers. 'Yahweh bless you!' they replied. [5]Boaz said to a servant of his who was in charge of the reapers, 'To whom does this young woman belong?' [6]And the servant in charge of the reapers replied, 'The girl is the Moabitess, the one who came back with Naomi from the Plains of Moab. [7]She said, "Please let me glean and pick up what falls from the sheaves behind the reapers." Thus she came, and here she stayed, with hardly a rest from morning until now.'

[8]Boaz said to Ruth, 'Listen to me, daughter. You must not go gleaning in any other field. You must not go away from here. Stay close to my work-women. [9]Keep your eyes on whatever part of the field they are reaping and follow behind. I have forbidden my men to molest you. And if you are thirsty, go to the pitchers and drink what the servants have drawn.' [10]Ruth fell on her face, prostrated herself and said, 'How have I attracted your favour, for you to notice me, who am only a foreigner?' [11]Boaz replied, 'I have been told all about the way you have behaved to your mother-in-law since your husband's death, and how you left your own father and mother and the land

where you were born to come to a people of whom you previously knew nothing. [12]May Yahweh repay you for what you have done, and may you be richly rewarded by Yahweh, the God of Israel, under whose wings you have come for refuge!' [13]She said, 'My lord, I hope you will always look on me with favour! You have comforted and encouraged me, though I am not even the equal of one of your work-women.'

[14]When it was time to eat, Boaz said to her, 'Come and eat some of this bread and dip your piece in the vinegar.' Ruth sat down beside the reapers and Boaz made a heap of roasted grain for her; she ate till her hunger was satisfied, and she had some left over. [15]When she had got up to glean, Boaz gave orders to his work-people, 'Let her glean among the sheaves themselves. Do not molest her. [16]And be sure you pull a few ears of corn out of the bundles and drop them. Let her glean them, and do not scold her.' [17]So she gleaned in the field till evening. Then she beat out what she had gleaned and it came to about a bushel of barley.

[18]Taking it with her, she went back to the town. Her mother-in-law saw what she had gleaned. Ruth also took out what she had kept after eating

all she wanted, and gave that to her. ¹⁹Her mother-in-law said, 'Where have you been gleaning today? Where have you been working? Blessed be the man who took notice of you!' Ruth told her mother-in-law in whose field she had been working. 'The name of the man with whom I have been working today', she said, 'is Boaz.' ²⁰Naomi said to her daughter-in-law, 'May he be blessed by Yahweh who does not withhold his faithful love from living or dead! This man', Naomi added, 'is a close relation of ours. He is one of those who have the right of redemption over us.' ²¹Ruth the Moabitess said to her mother-in-law, 'He also said, "Stay with my work-people until they have finished my whole harvest."' ²²Naomi said to Ruth, her daughter-in-law, 'It is better for you, daughter, to go with his work-women than to go to some other field where you might be ill-treated.' ²³So she stayed with Boaz's work-women, and gleaned until the barley and wheat harvests were finished. And she went on living with her mother-in-law.

BOAZ SLEEPS

3 Her mother-in-law Naomi then said, 'Daughter, is it not my duty to see you happily settled? ²And Boaz, the man with whose work-women you were, is he not our kinsman? Tonight he will be winnowing the barley on the threshing-floor. ³So wash and perfume yourself, put on your cloak and go down to the threshing-floor. Don't let him recognise you while he is still eating and drinking. ⁴But when he lies down, take note where he lies, then go and turn back the covering at his feet and lie down yourself. He will tell you what to do.' ⁵Ruth said, 'I shall do everything you tell me.'

⁶So she went down to the threshing-floor and did everything her mother-in-law had told her. ⁷When Boaz had finished eating and drinking, he went off happily and lay down beside the pile of barley. Ruth then quietly went, turned back the covering at his feet and lay down. ⁸In the middle of the night, he woke up with a shock and looked about him; and there lying at his feet was a woman. ⁹'Who are you?' he said; and she replied, 'I am your

servant Ruth. Spread the skirt of your cloak over your servant for you have the right of redemption over me.' ¹⁰'May Yahweh bless you, daughter,' he said, 'for this second act of faithful love of yours is greater than the first, since you have not run after young men, poor or rich. ¹¹Don't be afraid, daughter, I shall do everything you ask, since the people at the gate of my town all know that you are a woman of great worth. ¹²But, though it is true that I have the right of redemption over you, you have a kinsman closer than myself. ¹³Stay here for tonight and, in the morning, if he wishes to exercise his right over you, very well, let him redeem you. But if he does not wish to do so, then as Yahweh lives, I shall redeem you. Lie here till morning.' ¹⁴So she lay at his feet till morning, but got up before the hour when one man can recognise another; and he thought, 'It must not be known that this woman came to the threshing-floor.' ¹⁵He then said, 'Let me have the cloak you are wearing, hold it out!' She held it out while he put six measures of barley into it and then loaded it on to her; and off she went to the town.

¹⁶When Ruth got home, her mother-in-law asked her, 'How did things go with you, daughter?'

She then told her everything that the man had done for her. [17]'He gave me these six measures of barley and said, "You must not go home empty-handed to your mother-in-law."' [18]Naomi said, 'Do nothing, daughter, until you see how things have gone; I am sure he will not rest until he has settled the matter this very day.'

BOAZ MARRIES RUTH

4 Boaz, meanwhile, had gone up to the gate and sat down, and the relative of whom he had spoken then came by. Boaz said to him, 'Here, my friend, come and sit down'; the man came and sat down. [2]Boaz then picked out ten of the town's elders and said, 'Sit down here'; they sat down. [3]Boaz then said to the man who had the right of redemption, 'Naomi, who has come back from the Plains of Moab, is selling the piece of land that belonged to our brother, Elimelech. [4]I thought I should tell you about this and say, "Acquire it in the presence of the men who are sitting here and in the presence of the elders of my people. If you want to use your right of redemption, redeem it; if you do not, tell me so that I know, for I am the only person to redeem it besides yourself, and I myself come after you." ' The man said, 'I am willing to redeem it.' ⁵Boaz then said, 'The day you acquire the field from Naomi, you also acquire Ruth the Moabitess, the wife of the man who has died, to perpetuate the dead man's name in his inheritance.' ⁶The man with the right of redemption then said, 'I cannot use my right of redemption without jeopardising my own inheritance. Since I cannot use my right of redemption, exercise the right yourself.'

⁷Now, in former times, it was the custom in Israel to confirm a transaction in matters of redemption or inheritance by one of the parties taking off his sandal and giving it to the other. This was how agreements were ratified in Israel. ⁸So, when the man with the right of redemption said to Boaz, 'Acquire it for yourself,' he took off his sandal.

⁹Boaz then said to the elders and all the people there, 'Today you are witnesses that from Naomi I acquire everything that used to belong to

Elimelech, and everything that used to belong to Mahlon and Chilion [10]and that I am also acquiring Ruth the Moabitess, Mahlon's widow, to be my wife, to perpetuate the dead man's name in his inheritance, so that the dead man's name will not be lost among his brothers and at the gate of his town. Today you are witnesses to this.' [11]All the people at the gate said, 'We are witnesses'; and the elders said, 'May Yahweh make the woman about to enter your family like Rachel and Leah who together built up the House of Israel.

> Grow mighty in Ephrathah,
> be renowned in Bethlehem!

[12]And through the children Yahweh will give you by this young woman, may your family be like the family of Perez, whom Tamar bore to Judah.'

[13]So Boaz took Ruth and she became his wife. And when they came together, Yahweh made her conceive and she bore a son. [14]And the women said to Naomi, 'Blessed be Yahweh who has not left you today without anyone to redeem you. May his name be praised in Israel! [15] The child will be a comfort to you and the prop of your old age, for he

has been born to the daughter-in-law who loves you and is more to you than seven sons.' [16]And Naomi, taking the child, held him to her breast; and she it was who looked after him.

[17]And the women of the neighbourhood gave him a name. 'A son', they said, 'has been born to Naomi,' and they called him Obed. This was the father of Jesse, the father of David.

THE GENEALOGY OF DAVID

[18]These are the descendants of Perez. Perez fathered Hezron, [19]Hezron fathered Ram, Ram fathered Amminadab, [20]Amminadab fathered Nahshon, Nahshon fathered Salmon, [21]Salmon fathered Boaz, Boaz fathered Obed, [22]Obed fathered Jesse, and Jesse fathered David.

JUDITH

THE CAMPAIGN OF HOLOFERNES

NEBUCHADNEZZAR AND ARPHAXAD

1 It was the twelfth year of Nebuchadnezzar who reigned over the Assyrians in the great city of Nineveh. Arphaxad was then reigning over the Medes in Ecbatana. ²He surrounded this city with walls of dressed stones three cubits thick and six cubits long, making the rampart seventy cubits high and fifty cubits wide. ³At the gates he placed towers one hundred cubits high and, at the foundations, sixty cubits wide, ⁴the gates themselves being seventy cubits high and forty wide to allow his forces to march out in a body and his infantry to parade freely.

⁵About this time King Nebuchadnezzar gave

battle to King Arphaxad in the great plain lying in the territory of Ragae. ⁶Supporting him were all the peoples from the highlands, all from the Euphrates and Tigris and Hydaspes, and those from the plains who were subject to Arioch, king of the Elymaeans. Thus many nations had mustered to take part in the battle of the Cheleoudites.

⁷Nebuchadnezzar king of the Assyrians sent a message to all the inhabitants of Persia, to all the inhabitants of the western countries, Cilicia, Damascus, Lebanon, Anti-Lebanon, to all those along the coast, ⁸to the peoples of Carmel, Gilead, Upper Galilee, the great plain of Esdraelon, ⁹to the people of Samaria and its outlying towns, to those beyond Jordan, as far away as Jerusalem, Bethany, Chelous, Kadesh, the river of Egypt, Tahpanhes, Rameses and the whole territory of Goshen, ¹⁰beyond Tanis too and Memphis, and to all the inhabitants of Egypt as far as the frontiers of Ethiopia. ¹¹But the inhabitants of these countries ignored the summons of Nebuchadnezzar king of the Assyrians and did not rally to him to make war. They were not afraid of him, since in their view he appeared isolated. Hence they sent his

ambassadors back with nothing achieved and in disgrace. ¹²Nebuchadnezzar was furious with all these countries. He swore by his throne and kingdom to take revenge on all the territories of Cilicia, Damascus and Syria, of the Moabites and of the Ammonites, of Judaea and Egypt as far as the limits of the two seas, and to ravage them with the sword.

THE CAMPAIGN AGAINST ARPHAXAD

¹³In the seventeenth year, he gave battle with his whole army to King Arphaxad and in this battle defeated him. He routed Arphaxad's entire army and all his cavalry and chariots; ¹⁴he occupied his towns and advanced on Ecbatana; he seized its towers and plundered its market places, reducing its former magnificence to a mockery. ¹⁵He later captured Arphaxad in the mountains of Ragae and, thrusting him through with his spears, destroyed him once and for all.

¹⁶He then retired with his troops and all who had joined forces with him: a vast horde of armed

men. Then he and his army gave themselves up to carefree feasting for a hundred and twenty days.

THE CAMPAIGN IN THE WEST

2 In the eighteenth year, on the twenty-second day of the first month, a rumour ran through the palace that Nebuchadnezzar king of the Assyrians was to have his revenge on all the countries, as he had threatened. ²Summoning his general staff and senior officers, he held a secret conference with them, and with his own lips pronounced utter destruction on the entire area. ³It was then decreed that everyone should be put to death who had not answered the king's appeal.

⁴When the council was over, Nebuchadnezzar king of the Assyrians sent for Holofernes, general-in-chief of his armies and subordinate only to himself. He said to him, ⁵'Thus speaks the Great King, lord of the whole world, "Go; take men of proven valour, about a hundred and twenty thousand foot soldiers and a strong company of horse with twelve thousand cavalrymen; ⁶then advance against all the western lands, since these

people have disregarded my call. [7]Bid them have earth and water ready, because in my rage I am about to march on them; the feet of my soldiers will cover the whole face of the earth, and I shall plunder it. [8]Their wounded will fill the valleys and the torrents, and rivers, blocked with their dead, will overflow. [9]I shall lead them captive to the ends of the earth. [10]Now go! Begin by conquering this whole region for me. If they surrender to you, hold them for me until the time comes to punish them. [11]But if they resist, look on no one with clemency, hand them over to slaughter and plunder throughout the territory entrusted to you. [12]For by my life and by the living power of my kingdom I have spoken. All this I shall do by my power. [13]And you, neglect none of your master's commands, act strictly according to my orders without further delay.'"

[14]Leaving the presence of his sovereign, Holofernes immediately summoned all the marshals, generals and officers of the Assyrian army [15]and detailed the picked troops as his master had ordered, about a hundred and twenty thousand men and a further twelve thousand mounted archers. [16]He organised these in the normal battle formation. [17]He

then secured vast numbers of camels, donkeys and mules to carry the baggage, and innumerable sheep, oxen and goats for food supplies. [18]Every man received full rations and a generous sum of gold and silver from the king's purse.

[19]He then set out for the campaign with his whole army, in advance of King Nebuchadnezzar, to overwhelm the whole western region with his chariots, his horsemen and his picked body of foot. [20]A motley gathering followed in his rear, as numerous as locusts or the grains of sand on the ground; there was no counting their multitude.

THE STAGES OF HOLOFERNES' ADVANCE

[21]Thus they set out from Nineveh and marched for three days towards the Plain of Bectileth. From Bectileth they went on to pitch camp near the mountains that lie to the north of Upper Cilicia. [22]From there Holofernes advanced into the highlands with his whole army, infantry, horsemen, chariots. [23]He cut his way through Put and Lud, carried away captive all the sons of Rassis and sons

of Ishmael living on the verge of the desert south of
Cheleon, ²⁴marched along the Euphrates, crossed
Mesopotamia, rased all the fortified towns
controlling the Wadi Abron and reached the sea.
²⁵Next he attacked the territories of Cilicia,
butchering all who offered him resistance, advanced
on the southern frontiers of Japheth, facing Arabia,
²⁶completely encircled the Midianites, burned their
tents and plundered their sheep-folds, ²⁷made his
way down to the Damascus plain at the time of the
wheat harvest, set fire to the fields, destroyed the
flocks and herds, sacked the towns, laid the
countryside waste and put all the young men to the
sword. ²⁸Fear and trembling seized all the coastal
peoples; those of Sidon and Tyre, those of Sur, Ocina
and Jamnia. The populations of Azotos and Ascalon
were panic-stricken.

3 They therefore sent envoys to him to sue for
peace, to say, ²'We are servants of the great
King Nebuchadnezzar; we lie prostrate before you.
Treat us as you think fit. ³Our cattle-farms, all our
land, all our wheat fields, our flocks and herds, all
the sheep-folds in our encampments are at your
disposal. Do with them as you please. ⁴Our towns
and their inhabitants too are at your service; go and

treat them as you think fit.' ⁵These men came to Holofernes and delivered the message as above.

⁶He then made his way down to the coast with his army and stationed garrisons in all the fortified towns, levying outstanding men there as auxiliaries. ⁷The people of these cities and of all the other towns in the neighbourhood welcomed him, wearing garlands and dancing to the sound of tambourines. ⁸But he demolished their shrines and cut down their sacred trees, carrying out his commission to destroy all local gods so that the nations should worship Nebuchadnezzar alone and people of every language and nationality should hail him as a god.

⁹Thus he reached the edge of Esdraelon, in the neighbourhood of Dothan, a village facing the great ridge of Judaea. ¹⁰He pitched camp between Geba and Scythopolis and stayed there a full month to re-provision his forces.

JUDAEA ON THE ALERT

4 When the Israelites living in Judaea heard how Holofernes, general-in-chief of

Nebuchadnezzar king of the Assyrians, had treated the various nations, plundering their temples and destroying them, ²they were thoroughly alarmed at his approach and trembled for Jerusalem and the Temple of the Lord their God. ³They had returned from captivity only a short time before, and the resettlement of the people in Judaea and the reconsecration of the sacred furnishings, of the altar, and of the Temple, which had been profaned, were of recent date.

⁴They therefore alerted the whole of Samaria, Kona, Beth-Horon, Belmain, Jericho, Choba, Aesora and the Salem valley. ⁵They occupied the summits of the highest mountains and fortified the villages on them; they laid in supplies for the coming war, as the fields had just been harvested. ⁶Joakim the high priest, resident in Jerusalem at the time, wrote to the inhabitants of Bethulia and of Betomesthaim, two towns facing Esdraelon, towards the plain of Dothan. ⁷He ordered them to occupy the mountain passes, the only means of access to Judaea, for there it would be easy for them to halt an attacking force, the narrowness of the approach not allowing men to advance more than two abreast. ⁸The Israelites carried out the orders of

Joakim the high priest and of the people's Council
of Elders in session at Jerusalem.

A NATION AT PRAYER

[9]All the men of Israel cried most fervently to God
and humbled themselves before him. [10]They, their
wives, their children, their cattle, all their resident
aliens, hired or slave, wrapped sackcloth round their
loins. [11]All the Israelites in Jerusalem, including
women and children, lay prostrate in front of the
Temple, and with ashes on their heads stretched
out their hands before the Lord. [12]They draped the
altar itself in sackcloth and fervently joined
together in begging the God of Israel not to let
their children be carried off, their wives distributed
as booty, the towns of their heritage destroyed, the
Temple profaned and desecrated for the heathen
to gloat over. [13]The Lord heard them and looked
kindly on their distress.

The people fasted for many days throughout
Judaea as well as in Jerusalem before the sanctuary
of the Lord Almighty. [14]Joakim the high priest and
all who stood before the Lord, the Lord's priests

and ministers, wore sackcloth round their loins as they offered the perpetual burnt offering and the votive and voluntary offerings of the people. [15]With ashes on their turbans they earnestly called on the Lord to look kindly on the House of Israel.

A COUNCIL OF WAR IN HOLOFERNES' CAMP

5 Holofernes, general-in-chief of the Assyrian army, received the intelligence that the Israelites were preparing for war, that they had closed the mountain passes, fortified all the high peaks and laid obstructions in the plains. [2]Holofernes was furious. He summoned all the princes of Moab, all the generals of Ammon and all the satraps of the coastal regions. [3]'Men of Canaan,' he said, 'tell me: what people is this that occupies the hill-country? What towns does it inhabit? How large is its army? What are the sources of its power and strength? Who is the king who rules it and commands its army? [4]Why have they disdained to wait on me, as all the western peoples have?'

⁵Achior, leader of all the Ammonites, replied, 'May my lord be pleased to listen to what your servant is going to say. I shall give you the facts about these mountain folk whose home lies close to you. You will hear no lie from the mouth of your servant. ⁶These people are descended from the Chaldaeans. ⁷They once came to live in Mesopotamia, because they did not want to follow the gods of their ancestors who lived in Chaldaea. ⁸They abandoned the way of their ancestors to worship the God of heaven, the God they learnt to acknowledge. Banished from the presence of their own gods, they fled to Mesopotamia where they lived for a long time. ⁹When God told them to leave their home and set out for Canaan, they settled there and accumulated gold and silver and great herds of cattle. ¹⁰Next, famine having overwhelmed the land of Canaan, they went down to Egypt where they stayed till they were well nourished. There they became a great multitude, a race beyond counting. ¹¹But the king of Egypt turned against them and exploited them by forcing them to make bricks; he degraded them, reducing them to slavery. ¹²They cried to their God, who struck the

entire land of Egypt with incurable plagues, and the Egyptians expelled them. [13]God dried up the Red Sea before them [14]and led them forward by way of Sinai and Kadesh-Barnea. Having driven off all the inhabitants of the desert, [15]they settled in the land of the Amorites and in their strength exterminated the entire population of Heshbon. Then, having crossed the Jordan, they took possession of all the hill-country, [16]driving out the Canaanites before them and the Perizzites, Jebusites, Shechemites and all the Girgashites, and lived there for many years. [17]All the while they did not sin before their God, prosperity was theirs, for they have a God who hates wickedness. [18]But when they turned from the path he had marked out for them some were exterminated in a series of battles, others were taken captive to a foreign land. The Temple of their God was rased to the ground and their towns were seized by their enemies. [19]Then having turned once again to their God, they came back from the places to which they had been dispersed and scattered, regained possession of Jerusalem, where they have their Temple, and reoccupied the hill-country which had been left deserted. [20]So, now, master and lord, if this people has committed any fault, if they have sinned against their God, let us first be sure that they really have this reason to fail, then advance and attack them. ²¹But if their nation is guiltless, my lord would do better to abstain, for fear that their Lord and God should protect them. We should then become the laughing-stock of the whole world.'

²²When Achior had ended this speech, all the people crowding round the tent began protesting. Holofernes' own senior officers, as well as all the coastal peoples and the Moabites, threatened to tear him limb from limb. ²³'Why should we be afraid of the Israelites? They are a weak and powerless people, quite unable to stand a stiff attack. ²⁴Forward! Advance! Your army, Holofernes our master, will swallow them in one mouthful!'

ACHIOR HANDED OVER TO THE ISRAELITES

6 When the uproar of those crowding round the council had subsided, Holofernes,

general-in-chief of the Assyrian army,
reprimanded Achior in front of the whole crowd
of foreigners and Ammonites. ²'Achior, who do
you think you are, you and the Ephraimite
mercenaries, playing the prophet like this with us
today, and trying to dissuade us from making war
on the people of Israel? You claim their God will
protect them. And who is God if not Nebuchadnezzar? He himself will display his power and
wipe them off the face of the earth, and their
God will certainly not save them. ³But we, his
servants, shall destroy them as easily as a single
individual. They can never resist the strength of
our cavalry. ⁴We shall burn them all. Their
mountains will be drunk with their blood and
their plains filled with their corpses. Far from
being able to resist us, every one of them will die;
thus says King Nebuchadnezzar, lord of the
whole world. For he has spoken, and his words
will not prove empty. ⁵As for you, Achior, you
Ammonite mercenary, who in a rash moment
said these words, you will not see my face again
until the day when I have taken my revenge on
this brood from Egypt. ⁶And then the swords of
my soldiers and the spears of my officers will

pierce your sides. You will fall among their wounded, the moment I turn on Israel. [7]My servants will now take you into the hill-country and leave you near one of the towns in the passes; [8]you will not die, until you share their ruin. [9]No need to look so sad if you cherish the secret hope that they will not be captured! I have spoken; none of my words will prove idle.'

[10]Holofernes having commanded his tent-orderlies to seize Achior, to take him to Bethulia and to hand him over to the Israelites, [11]the orderlies took him, escorted him out of the camp and across the plain, and then, making for the hill-country, reached the springs below Bethulia. [12]As soon as the men of the town sighted them, they snatched up their weapons, left the town and made for the mountain tops, while all the slingers pelted them with stones to prevent them from coming up. [13]However, they managed to take cover at the foot of the slope, where they bound Achior and left him lying at the bottom of the mountain and returned to their master.

[14]The Israelites then came down from their town, stopped by him, unbound him and took him to Bethulia, where they brought him before

the chief men of the town, [15]who at that time were Uzziah son of Micah of the tribe of Simeon, Chabris son of Gothoniel and Charmis son of Melchiel. [16]These summoned all the elders of the town. The young men and the women also hurried to the assembly. Achior was made to stand with all the people surrounding him, and Uzziah questioned him about what had happened. [17]He answered by telling them what had been said at Holofernes' council, and what he himself had said in the presence of the Assyrian leaders, and how Holofernes had bragged of what he would do to the House of Israel. [18]At this the people fell to the ground and worshipped God. [19]'Lord God of heaven,' they cried, 'take notice of their arrogance and have pity on the humiliation of our race. Look kindly today on those who are consecrated to you.' [20]They then spoke reassuringly to Achior and praised him warmly. [21]After the assembly Uzziah took him home and gave a banquet for the elders; all that night they called on the God of Israel for help.

THE SEIGE OF BETHULIA

THE CAMPAIGN AGAINST ISRAEL

7 The following day Holofernes issued orders to his whole army and to the whole host of auxiliaries who had joined him, to break camp and march on Bethulia, to occupy the mountain passes and so open the campaign against the Israelites. ²The troops broke camp that same day. The actual fighting force numbered one hundred and twenty thousand infantry and twelve thousand cavalry, not to mention the baggage train with the vast number of men on foot concerned with that. ³They penetrated the valley in the neighbourhood of Bethulia, near the spring, and deployed on a wide front from Dothan to Balbaim and, in depth, from Bethulia to Cyamon, which faces Esdraelon. ⁴When the Israelites saw this horde, they were all appalled and said to each other, 'Now they will lick the whole country clean. Not even the loftiest peaks, the gorges or the hills will be able to stand the weight of them.' ⁵Each man snatched up his arms; they lit beacons on their towers and spent the whole night on watch.

⁶On the second day Holofernes deployed his entire cavalry in sight of the Israelites in Bethulia. ⁷He reconnoitred the slopes leading up to the town, located the water-points, seized them and posted pickets over them and returned to the main body. ⁸The chieftains of the sons of Esau, all the leaders of the Moabites and the generals of the coastal district then came to him and said, ⁹'If our master will be pleased to listen to us, his forces will not sustain a single wound. ¹⁰These Israelites do not rely so much on their spears as on the height of the mountains where they live. And admittedly it is not at all easy to scale these heights of theirs.

¹¹'This being the case, master, avoid engaging them in a pitched battle and then you will not lose a single man. ¹²Stay in camp, keep all your troops there too, while your servants seize the spring which rises at the foot of the mountain, ¹³since that is what provides the population of Bethulia with their water supply. Thirst will then force them to surrender their town. Meanwhile, we and our men

will climb the nearest mountain tops and form advance posts there to prevent anyone from leaving the town. [14]Hunger will waste them, with their wives and children, and before the sword can reach them they will already be lying in the streets outside their houses. [15]And you will make them pay dearly for their defiance and their refusal to meet you peaceably.'

[16]Their words pleased Holofernes as well as all his officers, and he decided to do as they suggested. [17]Accordingly, a troop of Moabites moved forward with a further five thousand Assyrians. They penetrated the valley and seized the Israelites' waterpoints and springs. [18]Meanwhile the Edomites and Ammonites went and took up positions in the highlands opposite Dothan, sending some of their men to the south-east opposite Egrebel near Chous on the Wadi Mochmur. The rest of the Assyrian army took up positions in the plain, covering every inch of the ground; their tents and equipment made an immense encampment, so vast were their numbers.

[19]The Israelites called on the Lord their God dispirited because the enemy had surrounded them and cut all line of retreat. [20]For thirty-four days the

Assyrian army, infantry, chariots, cavalrymen, had them surrounded. Every water-jar the inhabitants of Bethulia had was empty, [21]their storage-wells were drying up; on no day could a man drink his fill, since their water was rationed. [22]Their little children pined away, the women and young men grew weak with thirst; they collapsed in the streets and gateways of the town; they had no strength left.

[23]Young men, women, children, the whole people thronged clamouring round Uzziah and the chief men of the town, shouting in the presence of the assembled elders, [24]"May God be judge between you and us! For you have done us great harm, by not suing for peace with the Assyrians. [25]And now there is no one to help us. God has delivered us into their hands to be prostrated before them in thirst and utter helpless-ness. [26]Call them in at once; hand the whole town over to be sacked by Holofernes' men and all his army. [27]After all, we should be much better off as their booty than we are now; no doubt we shall be enslaved, but at least we shall be alive and not see our little ones dying before our eyes or our wives and children perishing. [28]By heaven and earth and by our God, the Lord of our fathers,

who is punishing us for our sins and the sins of our ancestors, we implore you to take this course now, today.' [29]Bitter lamentations rose from the whole assembly, and they all cried loudly to the Lord God.

[30]Then Uzziah spoke to them, 'Take heart, brothers! Let us hold out five days more. By then the Lord our God will take pity on us, for he will not desert us altogether. [31]At the end of this time, if no help is forthcoming, I shall do as you have said.' [32]With that he dismissed the people to their various quarters. The men went to man the walls and towers of the town, sending the women and children home. The town was full of despondency.

JUDITH

DESCRIPTION OF JUDITH

8 Judith was informed at the time of what had happened. She was the daughter of Merari son of Ox, son of Joseph, son of Oziel, son of Elkiah, son of Ananias, son of Gideon, son of Raphaim, son of Ahitub, son of Elijah, son of Hilkiah, son of Eliab, son of Nathanael, son of Salamiel, son of Sarasadai, son of Israel. [2]Her husband Manasseh, of her own tribe and family, had died at the time of the barley harvest. [3]He was supervising the men as they bound up the sheaves in the field when he caught sunstroke and had to take to his bed. He died in Bethulia, his home town, and was buried with his ancestors in the field that lies between Dothan and Balamon. [4]As a widow, Judith stayed inside her home for three years and four months. [5]She had had an upper room built for herself on the roof. She wore sackcloth next to the skin and dressed in widow's weeds. [6]She fasted every day of her widowhood except for the Sabbath eve, the Sabbath itself, the eve of New Moon, the feast of New Moon and the joyful festivals of the House of Israel. [7]Now she was very beautiful, charming to see. Her husband Manasseh had left her gold and silver, menservants and maidservants, herds and land; and she lived among all her possessions [8]without anyone finding a word to say against her, so devoutly did she fear God.

JUDITH AND THE ELDERS

[9]Hearing how the water shortage had demoralised the people and how they had complained bitterly to the headman of the town, and being also told what Uzziah had said to them and how he had given them his oath to surrender the town to the Assyrians in five days' time, [10]Judith immediately sent the serving-woman who ran her household to summon Chabris and Charmis, two elders of the town. [11]When these came in she said:

'Listen to me, leaders of the people of Bethulia. You were wrong to speak to the people as you did today and to bind yourself by oath, in defiance of God, to surrender the town to our enemies if the Lord did not come to your help within a set number of days. [12]Who are you, to put God to the test today, you, of all people, to set yourselves above him? [13]You put the Lord Almighty to the test! You do not understand anything, and never will. [14]If you cannot sound the depths of the human heart or unravel the arguments of the human mind, how can you fathom the God who made all things, or sound his mind or unravel his purposes? No brothers, do not provoke the anger of the Lord our

God. [15]Although it may not be his will to help us within the next five days, he has the power to protect us for as many days as he pleases, just as he has the power to destroy us before our enemies. [16]But you have no right to demand guarantees where the designs of the Lord our God are concerned. For God is not to be threatened as a human being is, nor is he, like a mere human, to be cajoled. [17]Rather, as we wait patiently for him to save, let us plead with him to help us. He will hear our voice if such is his good pleasure.

[18]'And indeed of recent times and still today there is not one tribe of ours, or family, or village, or town that has worshipped gods made by human hand, as once was done, [19]which was the reason why our ancestors were delivered over to sword and sack, and perished in misery at the hands of our enemies. [20]We for our part acknowledge no other God but him; and so we may hope he will not look on us disdainfully or desert our nation.

[21]'If indeed they capture us, as you expect, then all Judaea will be captured too, and our holy places plundered, and we shall answer with our blood for their profanation. [22]The slaughter of our brothers, the captivity of our country, the unpeopling of our

heritage, will recoil on our own heads among the nations whose slaves we shall become, and our new masters will look down on us as an outrage and a disgrace; [23]for our surrender will not reinstate us in their favour; no, the Lord our God will make it a thing to be ashamed of. [24]So now, brothers, let us set an example to our brothers, since their lives depend on us, and the sanctuary—Temple and altar—rests on us.

[25]'All this being so, let us rather give thanks to the Lord our God who, as he tested our ancestors, is now testing us. [26]Remember how he treated Abraham, all the ordeals of Isaac, all that happened to Jacob in Syrian Mesopotamia while he kept the sheep of Laban, his mother's brother. [27]For as these ordeals were intended by him to search their hearts, so now this is not vengeance that God is exacting on us, but a warning inflicted by the Lord on those who are near his heart.'

[28]Uzziah replied, 'Everything you have just said comes from an honest heart and no one will contradict a word of it. [29]Not that today is the first time your wisdom has been displayed; from your earliest years all the people have known how shrewd you are and of how sound a heart. [30]But,

parched with thirst, the people forced us to act as we had promised them and to bind ourselves by an inviolable oath. ³¹You are a devout woman; pray to the Lord, then, to send us a downpour to fill our storage-wells, so that our faintness may pass.'

³²Judith replied, 'Listen to me, I intend to do something, the memory of which will be handed down to the children of our race from age to age. ³³Tonight you must be at the gate of the town. I shall make my way out with my attendant. Before the time fixed by you for surrendering the town to our enemies, the Lord will make use of me to rescue Israel. ³⁴You must not ask what I intend to do; I shall not tell you until I have done it.' ³⁵Uzziah and the chief men said, 'Go in peace. May the Lord show you a way to take revenge on our enemies.' ³⁶And leaving the upper room they went back to their posts.

JUDITH'S PRAYER

9 Judith threw herself face to the ground, scattered ashes on her head, undressed as far as the sackcloth she was wearing and cried loudly to the Lord. At the same time in Jerusalem the evening incense was being offered in the Temple of God. Judith said:

2 Lord, God of my ancestor Simeon,
  you armed him with a sword
    to take vengeance on the foreigners
  who had undone a virgin's belt
    to her shame,
  laid bare her thigh to her confusion,
  violated her womb to her dishonour,
  since, though you said,
    'This must not be,' they did it.
3 For this you handed their leaders
    over to slaughter,
  and their bed, defiled by their treachery,
  was itself betrayed in blood.
  You struck the slaves with the chieftains
  and the chieftains with their retainers.
4 You left their wives to be carried off,
  their daughters to be taken captive,
  and their spoils to be shared out
  among the sons you loved,
  who had been so zealous for you,

had loathed the stain put on their blood
and called on you for help.

O God, my God,
now hear this widow too;
5 for you have made the past,
and what is happening now,
    and what will follow.
What is, what will be, you have planned;
what has been, you designed.
6 Your purposes stood forward;
'See, here we are!' they said.
For all your ways are prepared
and your judgements
    delivered with foreknowledge.
7 See the Assyrians,
    with their army abounding
glorying in their horses and their riders,
exulting in the strength of their infantry.
Trust as they may in shield and spear,
in bow and sling,
in you they have not recognised the Lord,
the breaker of battle-lines;
8 yours alone is the title of Lord.

Break their violence with your might,
in your anger bring down their strength.
For they plan to profane your holy places,
to defile the tabernacle,

the resting place of your glorious name,
and to hack down the horn of your altar.

⁹ Observe their arrogance,
send your fury on their heads,
give the strength I have in mind
to this widow's hand.

¹⁰ By guile of my lips
strike down slave with master,
and master with retainer.
Break their pride
by a woman's hand.

¹¹ Your strength does not lie in numbers,
nor your might in strong men;
since you are the God of the humble,
the help of the oppressed,
the support of the weak,
the refuge of the forsaken,
the Saviour of the despairing.

¹² Please, please, God of my father,
God of the heritage of Israel,
Master of heaven and earth,

Creator of the waters,
King of your whole creation,
hear my prayer.

13 Give me a beguiling tongue
to wound and kill
those who have formed such cruel designs
against your covenant,
against your holy dwelling-place,
against Mount Zion,
against the house belonging to your sons.

14 And demonstrate to every nation,
every tribe,
that you are the Lord,
God of all power, all might,
and that the race of Israel
has no protector but you.

JUDITH AND HOLOFERNES

JUDITH GOES TO THE CAMP OF HOLOFERNES

10 Thus Judith called on the God of Israel. When she had finished praying, [2]she got up from the floor, summoned her maid and went down into the rooms which she used on Sabbath days and festivals. [3]There she removed the sackcloth she was wearing and taking off her widow's dress, she washed all over, anointed herself plentifully with perfumes, dressed her hair, wrapped a turban round it and put on the robe of joy she used to wear when her husband Manasseh was alive. [4]She put sandals on her feet, put on her necklaces, bracelets, rings, earrings and all her jewellery, and made herself beautiful enough to beguile the eye of any man who saw her. [5]Then she handed her maid a skin of wine and a flask of oil, filled a bag with barley girdle-cakes, cakes of dried fruit and pure loaves, and wrapping all these provisions up gave them to her as well. ⁶They then went out, making for the town gate of Bethulia. There they found Uzziah waiting with the two elders of the town, Chabris and Charmis. ⁷When they saw Judith, her face so changed and her clothes so different, they were lost in admiration of her beauty. They said to her:

> ⁸May the God of our ancestors
>   keep you in his favour!
> May he crown your designs with success
> to the glory of the children of Israel,
> to the greater glory of Jerusalem!

⁹Judith worshipped God, and then she said, 'Have the town gate opened for me so that I can go out and fulfil all the wishes you expressed to me.' They did as she asked and gave orders to the young men to open the gate for her. ¹⁰This done, Judith went out accompanied by her maid, while the men of the town watched her all the way down the mountain and across the valley, until they lost sight of her.

[11]As the women were making straight through the valley, an advance unit of Assyrians intercepted them, [12]and, seizing Judith, began to question her. 'Which side are you on? Where do you come from? Where are you going?' 'I am a daughter of the Hebrews,' she replied, 'and I am fleeing from them since they will soon be your prey. [13]I am on my way to see Holofernes, the general of your army, to give him trustworthy information. I shall show him the road to take if he wants to capture all the hill-country without losing one man or one life.' [14]As the men listened to what she was saying, they stared in astonishment at the sight of such a beautiful woman. [15]'It will prove the saving of you,' they said to her, 'coming down to see our master of your own accord. You had better go to his tent; some of our men will escort you and hand you over to him. [16]Once you are in his presence do not be afraid. Tell him what you have just told us and you will be well treated.' [17]They then detailed a hundred of their men as escort for herself and her attendant, and these led them to the tent of Holofernes.

[18]News of her coming had already spread through the tents, and there was a general stir in

the camp. She was still outside the tent of Holofernes waiting to be announced, when a crowd began forming round her. [19]They were immediately impressed by her beauty and impressed with the Israelites because of her. 'Who could despise a people who have women like this?' they kept saying. 'Better not leave one of them alive; let any go and they could twist the whole world round their fingers!'

[20]The bodyguard and adjutants of Holofernes then came out and led Judith into the tent. [21]Holofernes was resting on his bed under a canopy of purple and gold studded with emeralds and precious stones. [22]The men announced her and he came out to the entrance to the tent, with silver torches carried before him.

[23]When Judith confronted the general and his adjutant, the beauty of her face astonished them all. She fell on her face and did homage to him, but his servants raised her from the ground.

THE FIRST MEETING OF JUDITH WITH HOLOFERNES

11 'Courage, woman,' Holofernes said, 'do not be afraid. I have never hurt anyone who chose to serve Nebuchadnezzar, king of the whole world. ²Even now, if your nation of mountain dwellers had not insulted me, I would not have raised a spear against them. This was their fault, not mine. ³But tell me, why have you fled from them and come to us? … Anyhow, this will prove the saving of you. Courage! You will live through this night, and many after. ⁴No one will hurt you. On the contrary, you will be treated as well as any who serve my lord King Nebuchadnezzar.'

⁵Judith said, 'Please listen favourably to what your slave has to say. Permit your servant to speak in your presence, I shall speak no word of a lie to my lord tonight. ⁶You have only to follow your servant's advice and God will bring your work to a successful conclusion; in what my lord undertakes he will not fail. ⁷Long life to Nebuchadnezzar, king of the whole world, who has sent you to set every living soul to rights; may his power endure! Since,

thanks to you, he is served not only by human beings, but because of your might the wild animals themselves, the cattle, and the birds of the air are to live in the service of Nebuchadnezzar and his whole House.

⁸'We have indeed heard of your genius and adroitness of mind. It is known everywhere in the world that throughout the empire you have no rival for ability, wealth of experience and brilliance in waging war. ⁹We have also heard what Achior said in his speech to your council. The men of Bethulia having spared him, he has told them everything that he said to you. ¹⁰Now, master and lord, do not disregard what he said; keep it in your mind, since it is true; our nation will not be punished, the sword will indeed have no power over them, unless they sin against their God. ¹¹But as it is, my lord need expect no repulse or setback, since death is about to fall on their heads, for sin has gained a hold over them, provoking the anger of their God each time that they commit it. ¹²As they are short of food and their water is giving out, they have resolved to fall back on their cattle and decided to make use of all the things that God has, by his laws, forbidden them to eat. ¹³Not only have

they made up their minds to eat the first-fruits of
corn and the tithes of wine and oil, though these
have been consecrated by them and set apart for
the priests who serve in Jerusalem in the presence
of our God, and may not lawfully even be handled
by ordinary people, ¹⁴but they have sent men to
Jerusalem—where the inhabitants are doing much
the same—to bring them back authorisation from
the Council of Elders. ¹⁵Now this will be the
outcome: when the permission arrives and they act
on it, that very day they will be delivered over to
you for destruction.

¹⁶'When I, your servant, came to know all this,
I fled from them. God has sent me to do things
with you at which the world will be astonished
when it hears. ¹⁷Your servant is a devout woman;
she honours the God of heaven day and night. I
therefore propose, my lord, to stay with you. I, your
servant, shall go out every night into the valley and
pray to God to let me know when they have
committed their sin. ¹⁸I shall then come and tell
you, so that you can march out with your whole
army; and none of them will be able to resist you.
¹⁹I shall be your guide right across Judaea until you
reach Jerusalem; there I shall enthrone you in the

very middle of the city. And then you can round them up like shepherd-less sheep, with never a dog daring to bark at you. Foreknowledge tells me this; this has been foretold to me and I have been sent to reveal it to you.'

²⁰Her words pleased Holofernes, and all his adjutants. Full of admiration at her wisdom they exclaimed, ²¹'There is no woman like her from one end of the earth to the other, so lovely of face and so wise of speech!' ²²Holofernes said, 'God has done well to send you ahead of the others. Strength will be ours, and ruin theirs who have insulted my lord. ²³As for you, you are as beautiful as you are eloquent; if you do as you have promised, your God shall be my God, and you yourself shall make your home in the palace of King Nebuchadnezzar and be famous throughout the world.'

12 With that he had her brought in to where his silver dinner service was already laid, and had his own food served to her and his own wine poured out for her. ²But Judith said, 'I would rather not eat this, in case I incur some fault. What I have brought will be enough for me.' ³'Suppose your provisions run out,'

Holofernes asked, 'how could we get more of the same sort? We have no one belonging to your race here.' [4]'May your soul live, my lord,' Judith answered, 'the Lord will have used me to accomplish his plan, before your servant has finished these provisions.' [5]Holofernes' adjutants then took her to a tent where she slept until midnight. A little before the morning watch, she got up. [6]She had already sent this request to Holofernes, 'Let my lord kindly give orders for your servant to be allowed to go out and pray,' [7]and Holofernes had ordered his guards not to prevent her. She stayed in the camp for three days; she went out each night to the valley of Bethulia and washed at the spring where the picket had been posted. [8]As she went she prayed to the Lord God of Israel to guide her in her plan to relieve the children of her people. [9]Having purified herself, she would return and stay in her tent until her meal was brought her in the evening.

JUDITH AT THE BANQUET OF HOLOFERNES

¹⁰On the fourth day Holofernes gave a banquet, inviting only his own staff and none of the other officers. ¹¹He said to Bagoas, the officer in charge of his personal affairs, 'Go and persuade that Hebrew woman you are looking after to come and join us and eat and drink in our company. ¹²We shall be disgraced if we let a woman like this go without seducing her. If we do not seduce her, everyone will laugh at us!' ¹³Bagoas then left Holofernes and went to see Judith. 'Would this young and lovely woman condescend to come to my lord?' he asked. 'She will occupy the seat of honour opposite him, drink the joyful wine with us and be treated today like one of the Assyrian ladies who stand in the palace of Nebuchadnezzar.' ¹⁴'Who am I', Judith replied, 'to resist my lord? I shall not hesitate to do whatever he wishes, and doing this will be my joy to my dying day.'

¹⁵So she got up and put on her dress and all her feminine adornments. Her maid preceded her, and on the floor in front of Holofernes spread the

fleece which Bagoas had given Judith for her daily
use to lie on as she ate.

¹⁶Judith came in and took her place. The heart
of Holofernes was ravished at the sight; his very
soul was stirred. He was seized with a violent
desire to sleep with her; and indeed since the first
day he saw her, he had been waiting for an
opportunity to seduce her. ¹⁷'Drink then!'
Holofernes said. 'Enjoy yourself with us!' ¹⁸'I am
delighted to do so, my lord, for since my birth I
have never felt my life more worthwhile than
today.' ¹⁹She took what her maid had prepared,
and ate and drank facing him. ²⁰Holofernes was
so enchanted with her that he drank far more
wine than he had drunk on any other day in his
life.

13 It grew late and his staff hurried away.
Bagoas closed the tent from the
outside, having shown out those who still lingered
in his lord's presence. They went to their beds
wearied with too much drinking, ²and Judith was
left alone in the tent with Holofernes who had
collapsed wine-sodden on his bed. ³Judith then
told her maid to stay just outside the bedroom and
wait for her to come out, as she did every morning.

She had let it be understood she would be going out to her prayers and had also spoken of her intention to Bagoas.

⁴By now everyone had left Holofernes, and no one, either important or unimportant, was left in the bedroom. Standing beside the bed, Judith murmured to herself:

> Lord God, to whom all strength belongs,
> prosper what my hands are now to do
> for the greater glory of Jerusalem;
> ⁵ now is the time to recover your heritage
> and to further my plans
> to crush the enemies arrayed against us.

⁶With that she went up to the bedpost by Holofernes' head and took down his scimitar; ⁷coming closer to the bed she caught him by the hair and said, 'Make me strong today, Lord God of Israel!' ⁸Twice she struck at his neck with all her might, and cut off his head. ⁹She then rolled his body off the bed and pulled down the canopy from the bedposts. After which, she went out and gave the head of Holofernes to her maid ¹⁰who put it in her food bag. The two then left the camp together, as they always did when

they went to pray. Once they were out of the camp, they skirted the ravine, climbed the slope to Bethulia and made for the gates.

JUDITH BRINGS THE HEAD OF HOLOFERNES TO BETHULIA

[11]From a distance, Judith shouted to the guards on the gates, 'Open the gate! Open! For the Lord our God is with us still, displaying his strength in Israel and his might against our enemies, as he has done today!' [12]Hearing her voice, the townsmen hurried down to the town gate and summoned the elders. [13]Everyone, great and small, came running down, since her arrival was unexpected. They threw the gate open, welcomed the women, lit a fire to see by and crowded round them. [14]Then Judith raised her voice and said, 'Praise God! Praise him! Praise the God who has not withdrawn his mercy from the House of Israel, but has shattered our enemies by my hand tonight!' [15]She pulled the head out of the bag and held it for them to see. 'This is the head of Holofernes, general-in-chief of the Assyrian army; here is the canopy under which he lay drunk! The

Lord has struck him down by the hand of a woman! [16]Glory to the Lord who has protected me in the course I took! My face seduced him, only to his own undoing; he committed no sin with me to shame me or disgrace me.'

[17]Overcome with emotion, the people all prostrated themselves and worshipped God, exclaiming with one voice, 'Blessings on you, our God, for confounding your people's enemies today!' [18]Uzziah then said to Judith:

> May you be blessed, my daughter,
>   by God Most High,
> beyond all women on earth;
> and blessed be the Lord God,
> Creator of heaven and earth,
> who guided you to cut off the head
> of the leader of our enemies!

[19] The trust which you have shown
> will not pass from human hearts,
> as they commemorate
> the power of God for evermore.

[20] God grant you may be
>   always held in honour
> and rewarded with blessings,

since you did not consider your own life
when our nation was brought
    to its knees,
but warded off our ruin,
walking in the right path before our God.
And the people all said, 'Amen! Amen!'

VICTORY

THE JEWS ATTACK THE ASSYRIAN CAMP

14 Judith said, 'Listen to me, brothers. Take this head and hang it on your battlements. ²When morning comes and the sun is up, let every man take his arms and every able-bodied man leave the town. Appoint a leader for them, as if you meant to march down to the plain against the Assyrian advanced post. But you must not do this. ³The Assyrians will gather up their equipment, make for their camp and wake up their commanders; they in turn will rush to the tent of

Holofernes and not be able to find him. They will then be seized with panic and flee at your advance. [4]All you and the others who live in the territory of Israel will have to do is to give chase and slaughter them as they retreat.

[5]'But before you do this, call me Achior the Ammonite, for him to see and identify the man who held the House of Israel in contempt, the man who sent him to us as someone already doomed to die.' [6]So they had Achior brought from Uzziah's house. No sooner had he arrived and seen the head of Holofernes held by a member of the people's assembly than he fell on his face in a faint. [7]They lifted him up. He then threw himself at Judith's feet and, prostrate before her, exclaimed:

> May you be blessed
>   in all the tents of Judah
> and in every nation;
>   those who hear your name
> will be seized with dread!

[8]'Now tell me everything that you have done in these past few days.' And surrounded by the people, Judith told him everything she had done from the

day she left Bethulia to the moment when she was speaking. [9]When she came to the end, the people cheered at the top of their voices until the town echoed. [10]Achior, recognising all that the God of Israel had done, believed ardently in him and, accepting circumcision, was permanently incorporated into the House of Israel.

[11]At daybreak they hung the head of Holofernes on the ramparts. Every man took his arms and they all went out in groups to the slopes of the mountain. [12]Seeing this, the Assyrians sent word to their leaders, who in turn reported to the generals, the captains of thousands and all the other officers; [13]and these in their turn reported to the tent of Holofernes. 'Rouse our master,' they said to his major-domo, 'these slaves have dared to march down on us to attack—and to be wiped out to a man!' [14]Bagoas went inside and struck the curtain dividing the tent, thinking that Holofernes was sleeping with Judith. [15]But as no one seemed to hear, he drew the curtain and went into the bedroom, to find him thrown down dead on the threshold, with his head cut off. [16]He gave a great shout, wept, sobbed, shrieked and rent his clothes. [17]He then went into the tent which Judith had

occupied and could not find her either. Then, rushing out to the men, he shouted, ¹⁸'The slaves have rebelled! A single Hebrew woman has brought shame on the House of Nebuchadnezzar. Holofernes is lying dead on the ground, without his head!'

¹⁹When they heard this, the leaders of the Assyrian army tore their tunics in consternation, and the camp rang with their wild cries and their shouting.

15 When the men who were still in their tents heard the news they were appalled. ²Panic-stricken and trembling, no two of them could keep together, the rout was complete, with one accord they fled along every track across the plain or through the mountains. ³The men who had been bivouacking in the mountains round Bethulia were fleeing too. Then all the Israelite warriors charged down on them. ⁴Uzziah sent messengers to Betomasthaim, Bebai, Choba, Kola, throughout the whole territory of Israel, to inform them of what had happened and to urge them all to hurl themselves on the enemy and annihilate them. ⁵As soon as the Israelites heard the news, they fell on them as one man and massacred them all the way

to Choba. The men of Jerusalem and the entire
mountain country also rallied to them, once they
had been informed of the events in the enemy
camp. Then the men of Gilead and Galilee attacked
them on the flank and struck at them fiercely till
they neared Damascus and its territory. ⁶All the
other inhabitants of Bethulia fell on the Assyrian
camp and looted it to their great profit. ⁷The
Israelites returning from the slaughter seized what
was left. The hamlets and villages of the mountain
country and the plain also captured a great deal of
booty, since there were vast stores of it.

THANKSGIVING

⁸Joakim the high priest and the entire Council of
Elders of Israel, who were in Jerusalem, came to
gaze on the benefits that the Lord had lavished on
Israel and to see Judith and congratulate her. ⁹On
coming to her house, they blessed her with one
accord, saying:

> You are the glory of Jerusalem!
> You are the great pride of Israel!

You are the highest honour of our race!
¹⁰ By doing all this with your own hand
you have deserved well of Israel,
and God has approved
what you have done.
May you be blessed by the Lord Almighty
in all the days to come!

And the people all said, 'Amen!'

¹¹The people looted the camp for thirty days. They gave Judith the tent of Holofernes, all his silver plate, his divans, his drinking bowls and all his furniture. She took this, loaded her mule, harnessed her carts and heaped the things into them. ¹²All the women of Israel, hurrying to see her, formed choirs of dancers in her honour. Judith took wands of vine-leaves in her hand and distributed them to the women who accompanied her; ¹³she and her companions put on wreaths of olive. Then she took her place at the head of the procession and led the women as they danced. All the men of Israel, armed and garlanded, followed them, singing hymns.

¹⁴With all Israel round her, Judith broke into this song of thanksgiving and the whole people sang this hymn:

16 Break into song for my God,
to the tambourine,
sing in honour of the Lord,
to the cymbal,
let psalm and canticle mingle for him,
extol his name, invoke it!

2 For the Lord is a God
who breaks battle-lines;
he has pitched his camp
in the middle of his people
to deliver me from the hands
of my oppressors.

3 Assyria came down
from the mountains of the north,
came with tens of thousands of his army.
Their multitude blocked the ravines,
their horses covered the hills.

4 He threatened to burn up my country,
destroy my young men with the sword,
dash my sucklings to the ground,
make prey of my little ones,
carry off my maidens;

5 but the Lord Almighty has thwarted them
by a woman's hand.

⁶ For their hero did not fall
    at the young men's hands,
it was not the sons of Titans
    struck him down,
no proud giants made that attack,
but Judith, the daughter of Merari,
who disarmed him
    with the beauty of her face.
⁷ She laid aside her widow's dress
to raise up those
    who were oppressed in Israel;
she anointed her face with perfume,
⁸ bound her hair under a turban,
put on a linen gown to seduce him.
⁹ Her sandal ravished his eye,
her beauty took his soul prisoner
and the scimitar cut through his neck!

¹⁰ The Persians trembled at her boldness,
the Medes were daunted by her daring.
¹¹ These were struck with fear
    when my lowly ones raised the war cry,
these were seized with terror
    when my weak ones shouted,
and when they raised their voices

        these gave ground.
¹² The children of mere girls
      ran them through,
pierced them
      like the offspring of deserters.
    They perished in the battle of my Lord!
¹³ I shall sing a new song to my God.
    Lord, you are great, you are glorious,
    wonderfully strong, unconquerable.
¹⁴ May your whole creation serve you!
    For you spoke and things came into being,
    you sent your breath
      and they were put together,
    and no one can resist your voice.

¹⁵ Should mountains be tossed
      from their foundations
  to mingle with the waves,
  should rocks melt
  like wax before your face,
  to those who fear you,
  you would still be merciful.

¹⁶ A little thing indeed
    is a sweetly smelling sacrifice,

still less the fat
burned for you in burnt offering;
but whoever fears the Lord
is great for ever.

[17] Woe to the nations
who rise against my race!
The Lord Almighty
will punish them on judgement day.
He will send fire and worms in their flesh
and they will weep with pain
for evermore.

[18]When they reached Jerusalem they fell on their faces before God and, once the people had been purified, they presented their burnt offerings, voluntary offerings and gifts. [19]All Holofernes' property given her by the people, and the canopy she herself had stripped from his bed, Judith vowed to God as a dedicated offering. [20]For three months the people gave themselves up to rejoicings in front of the Temple in Jerusalem, where Judith stayed with them.

JUDITH LIVES TO OLD AGE. HER DEATH

[21]When this was over, everyone returned home. Judith went back to Bethulia and lived on her property; as long as she lived, she enjoyed a great reputation throughout the country. [22]She had many suitors, but all her days, from the time her husband Manasseh died and was gathered to his people, she never gave herself to another man. [23]Her fame spread more and more, the older she grew in her husband's house; she lived to the age of one hundred and five. She emancipated her maid, then died in Bethulia and was buried in the cave where Manasseh her husband lay. [24]The House of Israel mourned her for seven days. Before her death she had distributed her property among her own relations and those of her husband Manasseh.

[25]Never again during the lifetime of Judith, nor indeed for a long time after her death, did anyone trouble the Israelites.